CARING FOR
Your Tropical Fish

Jake Sharman

Cats are relatively easy pets to care for since they're very independent, but of course they still need to be groomed and their litter box emptied at least once per week, if not more. With cats, you also need to be mindful of when they're outside, as it's not unusual for them to get injured or to bring home dead animals and other "surprises" that you would really rather not deal with. They also definitely need to be spayed or neutered, or else you find yourself with even more cats than you imagined.

Of course, none of this happens with fish. They don't need to be walked, groomed, scooped up after, and don't get into fights with other neighborhood fish. They won't leave dead mice on the doorstep and never get fleas.

Fish are also some of the most inexpensive pets you'll ever have. It's true that a new aquarium, especially a larger one, can be quite costly but used aquariums can usually be found just about anywhere and there is no end to the variety of sizes you can purchase as well. And while it may cost a few dollars to properly equip your aquarium with a pump, filter, and so on, once you have these things in place they usually last for years.

Fish of course require food and other additives for their environment, but nowhere near the quantities of other pets. When was the last time you saw someone come home with a twenty-pound bag of fish food slung over their shoulder? People of just about any budget can afford fish.

A True Work of Art

Probably everyone wants a home or living space that is truly unique just to them, and many homeowners spend hours picking out just the right artwork, furniture, and accessories.

Tropical fish in a beautiful aquarium can make your home feel warm, personal, and homey, and very unique just to you. They can also be conversation pieces, something to keep you and your guests occupied for an entire evening. Picking out an aquarium and selection of tropical fish can really express your own personality and tastes the way no other work of art really can!

A Perfect Fit

Do you live in an apartment where you are not allowed pets? Chances are that fish are an exception to this rule, since they won't leave a mess on the carpet and won't make noise when the neighbors come home. As a matter of fact, most landlords don't even realize when a person has fish in their home!

They may restrict sizes of aquariums especially for second floor apartments in case of a leak or breakage, but for the most part a tenant can have a smaller aquarium in virtually any place they care to live.

This is also something to think about if you live in very tight or cramped quarters. Not everyone is blessed with thousands of square feet for their home, and if you have a family you need to be mindful of your space as well. Larger dogs and several cats just don't seem to fit right in those cramped quarters, but a small aquarium can be fit into any corner in virtually any space. Fish also won't be getting under your feet as you do your chores, won't get in your lap when you're trying to watch television, and won't assault you at the door when you come home.

Oh, the Variety

Sure, there's an endless variety of cats and dogs that you can pick from, but keep in mind that very often dogs and cats just don't get along with one another. Dogs need to assert dominance and cats often fight viciously over territory and to be independent.

Tropical fish also come in an endless variety of colors, shapes and sizes, and never fight for dominance or territory.

Planning a good aquarium is like planning a garden - you can mix and match and plan what colors you want! Many people who are educated about tropical fish find it a big part of the joy of owning them when they can mix and match the different breeds and colors, and find that they have a collection that is eye-catching and truly a joy to watch.

Some who learn about tropical fish also find that some are more of a challenge to keep than others, and they view it as an accomplishment to keep one for the maximum lifespan it has. This is also much like a gardener that enjoys not just planting in the spring but in nurturing their little flowers all summer long.

Educational

Who do you think has more knowledge of horses, those who read books about them or those who live on a horse farm?

Who do you think knows more about the Grand Canyon, someone that has seen it in picture books or someone that actually lives in one of its nearby cities?

Who do you think knows more about children, those who are actually parents or those who have just read the latest magazines about parenting?

Obviously those who have a hands-on situation are probably going to know more about something, and have a deeper appreciation for it, than someone that has just read about these things in book. You can read all the travel brochures you want, but until you're actually standing in that tropical paradise with your toes buried in the white sand and smelling the salt air, or until you're sitting in a local restaurant having a meal prepared by authentic area chefs, you're not really going to appreciate that particular location. We can learn a lot about anything by reading books, but it's the personal touch that makes things so much more real to us and that really deepens our appreciation for whatever that is - an animal, a location, a foreign country, and so on.

What's the point? Well think about your kids for a moment. It's one thing to have them read books about nature and the environment and what it's like to care for a pet or an animal; it's good to talk about conservation and pollution and how these things affect living creatures in different areas; it's quite another thing to give them a hands-on experience with these circumstances.

Tropical fish are like a tiny ecosystem that you keep in your own home. Of course a dog or a cat can teach a child about responsibility, companionship, taking care of an animal, and so on, but fish give you so much more. When the tank isn't cleaned properly it becomes cloudy - a perfect illustration of what pollution does to lakes, rivers, oceans, and the environment overall!

They can also see how mold and fungus grow rapidly, how mollusks cling to the side of glass, and so on. They learn firsthand what a delicate balance our entire environment is when it comes to water, oxygen, and light, and how these things must in good order for all species and varieties of life to survive.

Having Tropical Fish

Realizing all these wonderful things about keeping fish is one thing; actually having fish in your own home and taking care of them properly is quite another matter. Fish are relatively easy to take care of but you can't just dump them in a tank of water and sprinkle some food on top once a day, not if you expect them to survive and thrive.

Maybe this is one reason why you've hesitated to get tropical fish even though you think they're beautiful to look at, know that they'll fit in your limited space, or would love for your kids to have firsthand experience with such a setup.

Or maybe you've had tropical fish in the past and have noticed that they haven't thrived the way you expected.

Maybe they've even died very prematurely, causing you a lot of frustration, irritation, and even grief. Fish are an investment and some of the more rare varieties can be very costly; not to mention the fact that it's easy to become as attached to them as you would any other pet or member of the family! When one dies it can be devastating.

But really, tropical fish don't need to be difficult when it comes to their care and keeping. Much like a garden, all one needs is some basic knowledge of each variety and what's required to keep the aquarium healthy. Other than that, the fish can take care of themselves the same way that flowers thrive on their own with just some basic care by the homeowner.

And this is where we come in. In this booklet, we will teach you:

- How to decide the best tank to get, whether glass or acrylic, and how large you should opt for.

- All the accessories you need for your tank, and will caution you against those you don't need and those where the cheaper model is just as good as any other.

- Some of the basic phrases and terms used in the world of tropical fish.

- How to set up your tank once you get it home, and what to look for to know you're ready to introduce fish.

- How to take care of your fish on an everyday basis, including the best things to feed them and how to take care of common illnesses and diseases, and how to create a perfect atmosphere for them to breed and procreate.
- How to help your fish breed.
- How to take care of your tank on an everyday basis, and how to correct common problems you may encounter with your tank including poor water quality, cloudiness, and other issues.
- Basic information about the most popular fish you can choose for your aquarium along with some warnings and cautions as well.
- The most basic way you can prepare for your fish and take care of them once you do welcome them in your home.

Some shy away from keeping tropical fish because they've been told that it's a complicated and difficult hobby and that if you don't get things just perfect your fish will all die. We say *hogwash*! Children can keep tropical fish and help them to not only live but to thrive as well. It takes just a few simply steps to get your tank ready for your fish and a few other simple steps to care for them once they're home.

So if you're ready to get started, well, so are we!

The Basics of Tropical Fish

Just what is meant by tropical fish, anyway? Does this refer to saltwater, freshwater, or what?

Understanding just what is meant by tropical fish, what varieties this entails, and learning a bit about their natural habitat is of course going to be the first step toward learning how to take care of them properly. In their native environment tropical fish thrive when they have the food and atmosphere they need and when humans don't interfere; learning about all those necessary elements that are important and learning about the things you need to avoid doing to harm them is going to go a long way toward helping you keep your fish healthy.

Terms to Remember

If you're going to care for your fish properly you need to remember some terms and phrases that relate to your fish. Understanding some of these basic terms is also going to help you in the care and feeding of them as well.

The tropics.

You may have a good grasp on what is meant by "the tropics," and you may immediately get an idea of a warm island or exotic location. However, if the term tropics referred only to a warm and sandy location, then by this definition the dessert is part of the tropics!

There is actually an area of the earth that is technically referred to as being part of the tropics. According to Wikipedia, "The tropics are the geographic region of the Earth where the sun passes through the zenith twice during the solar year (once as the sun appears to go north and once as it appears to go south). At the limits, called the tropics of Cancer and Capricorn, this occurs once at the relevant solstice.

This area is centered on the equator and limited in latitude by the Tropic of Cancer in the northern hemisphere, at approximately 23°26' (23.4°) N latitude, and the Tropic of Capricorn in the southern hemisphere at 23°26' (23.4°) S latitude. This region is also referred to as the tropical zone and the torrid zone."

Of course definitions are often flexible and up for grabs; if someone says that they have tropical fish from some area of the world that falls outside this red zone, there's no need to start a debate! In general terms the tropics can refer to any area with a mostly warm and humid climate and lush vegetation.

Also, there are areas of the world that actually fall within this band that are anything but "tropical," including Mt. Kilimanjaro, the Australian Outback, and the Sahara Desert.

Tropical fish.

The term "tropical fish" just refers to fish species that are native to tropical areas of the world, and this may mean both *freshwater* and *saltwater* species.

This may come as a surprise to many who assume that tropical fish are only those of the saltwater varieties, but it's actually the opposite that's generally true. Fish keepers often use the term tropical fish to refer to only those requiring fresh water, whereas saltwater fish are commonly referred to as *marine fish*.

Aquarium cycling.

We'll get into setting up and taking care of your aquarium in a later section, but aquarium cycling generally refers to getting all the elements of your aquarium right before you add your fish. To survive and thrive, fish need a healthy environment that includes bacteria, nitrates, and a proper pH level. These things don't happen overnight and they don't happen by just dumping tap water into your tank either.
Many enthusiasts are anxious to start adding fish on day one, but this process of aquarium cycling is vitally important before those fish should be dumped in.

The nitrogen cycle.

The nitrogen cycle is something that actually goes on in every part of the environment but which is incredibly important when it comes to fish and a fish tank, which cannot process as many chemicals and chemical reactions as readily and easily as areas with fresh air can. Nitrogen and other chemicals get caught in the water and cannot escape as it should, and adjustments sometimes need to be made.

While fish are very hardy, they're obviously not indestructible and are as sensitive to their environment as humans are. Imagine living in a very heavily polluted area from which you can never get relief - this can happen to fish when the nitrogen cycle in their tank is ignored.

Dropsy.

Dropsy is a disease that works on the internal organs of your fish.

We'll discuss in a later section the importance of caring for your fish' health and exactly how to do so, but anyone that's trying to care for tropical fish should be familiar with this term as it is one of the most common diseases to attack kill tropical fish.

Planted tank.

If you've ever done any diving, fishing, or have even taken a walk along the beach, you know that fish are not the only living creatures underneath the water. While we may use the blanket term "seaweed" to apply to plants and vegetation that grow under water, there are actually dozens of varieties of plants that grow very well in water.

Having a planted tank means introducing vegetation to your tank along with fish. It's important to have an understanding of what these plants are so that they will not only thrive in your tank but so that you are having the right mix of plants and fish as well. Too many plants will mean that they are upsetting the delicate chemical balance of your tank, but not enough will mean that your fish are not getting the important elements they're releasing as well. You need to be sure that you're not crowding your fish but are providing for them properly.

Species only tanks.

We'll discuss in a later section the many varieties of fish there are and some things to consider before adding any of them, but there are a few different common species of fish that most hobbyists consider.

Each species has its own sensitivity to temperature, pH, and so on.

Some are very hearty and not as finicky whereas others are extremely sensitive and even temperamental to other fish. Having a species only tank means that you are keeping only one particular species of fish in your tank so that you know exactly what temperature to keep it, the proper pH the fish need, and are more assured that they will interact well with one another. You'll hear this expression a lot in certain circles and when purchasing your fish, so it's important to educate yourself about what species your choices are and whether or not they should be kept in a species only tank or will work well with a variety of fish.

Absorption.

This refers to your filter medium trapping unwanted materials; it does this through absorption, that is, it pulls water through the filter part and absorbs the things that are not part of the water.

Air stone.

This is a device that is attached to an air pump to produce various bubble effects. Tanks don't always need air pumps and usually these are added just for the visual effect of bubbles, and adding an air stone or different air stones will produce different bubble effects.

Depending on your budget for such accessories and how visually interesting you want your tank to be, you may purchase one of these or forego it altogether.

Hard water.

If you have hard water, your water has a high concentration of dissolved salts in it. Many people have hard tap water and can notice this by the residue it leaves on showerheads and around the sink; some tap water systems are treated with agents that dissolve this salt but if you're using tap water that's hard for your tank you're going to have hard water in your tank. Sometimes this can be a problem but often it's not enough to affect your fish; we'll discuss in a later section how to differentiate and what to do about this problem.

Fry.

Baby fish that are fully formed. Interestingly this may be where we get the slang term "small fry" for human children!

Ballast.

A transformer which changes the voltage from your house outlet to the voltage needed to power different types of lighting. You may or may not need this for larger tanks that require more powerful forms of lighting; usually the tank kit or lighting kit will include it or inform you if it's needed.

Breeding or quarantine tank.

This is a separate tank that closely mimics the conditions of the large tank and is meant for fish that need to be separated, such as those that are sick or that you are trying to breed. Some fish need to be separated from other fish in order for successful breeding so sometimes a quarantine tank needs to be set up for them.

A quarantine or breeding tank can be much smaller than your regular tank of course and usually just needs the basics of substrate, a few plants, and a small heater and filter. Since it's only used on a temporary basis and only for one or two fish at a time it doesn't need to be as ornate or elaborate as your typical tank.

Metal halide.

A very intense type of light sometimes used for marine fish. We'll discuss lighting types and strategies in a later section but keep in mind that metal halide is very rarely needed for home tanks.

If a salesperson tries to sell you metal halide, consider the cost difference and you'll realize why. Typically fluorescent lights are all that's needed, but more on that later.

Types of Fish

Having a basic understanding of the different types of tropical fish that are commonly available is going to help you out tremendously; most species have their own behavior characteristics and some interact well with other species while some don't. Let's get a basic overview of these different types of fish here.

Good cleaner fish for your aquarium are catfish. They are algae eaters and stick to the bottom of any tank. They're not usually the most attractive fish there are but can offer a good contrast to your more colorful fish. They can also grow to be quite large so you do need an appropriate tank.

There are thousands of varieties of cichlids and they are a very popular option for aquariums because of this variety and because of their unique behavior and temperament.

Anabantoids are also known as labyrinth fish and these are comprised of Gouramis, Bettas (fighting fish), and Climbing Perch. They are typically very sturdy fish and survive in oxygen-poor environments.

Killifish are some of the most stunning tropical fish that you'll find. However some have very short life spans of around six months or so; be careful when purchasing these varieties.

Discus are popular tropical fish but are usually called Kings of Aquarium Fish because they are very demanding, territorial, and can be very expensive as well. They have been bred quite a bit by aquarium enthusiasts so are typically available in any variety of colors and designs.

Characins are the very popular tetras. They are considered an essential inclusion and staple to most home tanks and are usually readily available and very affordable. This group however includes piranhas and other dangerous varieties so be sure you know what you're getting when you shop!

Livebearers include the platies, swordtails, guppies and mollies. These too are considered staples of aquarium tropical fish. There are many different varieties, sizes, and colors from which to choose and they are typically very peaceful and calm fish and so make a great addition to any tank or aquarium.

Oddballs are the fish that don't quite fit into any of these categories. It might not be the nicest term to use when referring to them, but we doubt that they're really that offended!

When purchasing your fish.

It's good to get as much education about your potential additions as you can. Some fish have quite a distinct personality and don't play well with others, if you get our drift. Make sure your mix of fish is going to be happy and healthy for all of them involved.

Understanding a few of these simple terms and phrases are important when it comes to caring for your tropical fish. But before you can ever introduce any of these great pets to your home, you need to have your tank in your home and set up appropriately. Let's go over that information now.

Purchasing Your Tank and Accessories

Welcome home!

As much as you may want to slap up such a sign on your tank and just start dumping those beautiful fish into your tank, consider how important it is to have it properly prepared for them before you bring them home. After all, when you purchase a new home or move into a new apartment, aren't you sure to have all the necessary utilities turned on and to have some furniture moved in before you get settled? So it is with your fish - they need a healthy environment from the very first minute they arrive, so this means you need to do some preparation well in advance of purchasing or bringing home the fish.

The Tank

Go to any pet supply store and browse the aquariums. What do you see? No doubt an endless variety of choices, all within a very wide price range. When you're considering tropical fish there are a few things you want to remember about what type of tank to purchase.

Get the biggest you can afford and fit in your home.

Being told to get the biggest and the best may seem like a cliché, but when it comes to tropical fish it's very good advice for the tank. Fish need a lot of room to swim around and they'll be sharing the tank with other fish and vegetation, all of which will be competing for precious chemicals needed to support their own life. When you have an environment that's enclosed like a tank, you want it to be as large as possible in order to properly support life.

Think of it this way. How many times have you heard about jail overcrowding? Cramming a number of prisoners into one cell is not healthy for any of them. Imagine if you had to spend time in an enclosed space - wouldn't you want it to be as large as possible? Not only is it healthier to have fresher air but it's just more comfortable to you physically.

The same goes for your fish. It's healthier and more comfortable for them to be in the largest space possible. If you can't afford a very large tank or can't fit it into your home, you're going to need to adjust your plans for the tank accordingly. This will mean less fish or smaller varieties and less vegetation as well.

It's also easier to take care of a larger fish tank than a smaller one. Water changes in larger tanks are done less often and there is less manual maintenance as well. Also, the more water you have in a tank the more it will help with problems you may encounter. For example, when a fish dies and is left in the tank for any length of time, this affects the chemicals in that tank. The less water you have, the more off balance those chemicals will become. But more water means that these changes will have less of an impact on the tank overall.

It may sound strange but sometimes larger tanks are actually more affordable than smaller ones. This is because they are mass produced and larger tanks use less expensive parts to produce. And if you're worried about the accessories needed for your tank, don't be. The accessories are usually very cheap and won't cost you that much extra for a larger tank than they will for a smaller one. So buy the biggest you can reasonably fit into your home and that you can afford. This will mean more fish and healthier ones as well.

Glass or acrylic?

Is there any difference between glass tanks and acrylic tanks when it comes to an aquarium? You may have heard that one is better than the other or that acrylic is actually dangerous. Let's explore this issue a bit further here, as there are pros and cons to both choices.

Acrylic aquariums are of course lighter than glass tanks, so if you're opting for something larger you may want to go with acrylic just for the sake of being able to move it, and of course the stand you use for your aquarium is going to be important too. Think of tanks as like television sets - the lighter ones can be on a lighter stand without incident but if you have a larger set that's very heavy on one of those old rickety media carts, you're going to have it topple. So the weight of the larger tanks is going to be a factor.

Acrylic tanks are harder to clean than glass and actually scratch easier. Depending on the time you can devote to keeping the tank clean and whether or not you have children that are going to be constantly tapping and scratching the tank, you need to consider these factors as well.

The good factors about acrylic are that they are actually more visually appealing than glass tanks since light filters better through acrylic than it does glass. They're also better for areas that are earthquake-prone or that are near airports or other areas that might cause vibrations.

Also, acrylic can be molded and formed into different shapes much easier than glass which means you can get tanks of various shapes with acrylic. If you want a tank in the shape of a hexagon or that's rounded you may want to opt for acrylic.

On the other hand, glass fish tanks are usually cheaper than acrylic because they're easier to produce. A plain square or rectangle glass tank is going to be your most affordable option. Since glass is harder to scratch than acrylic you would do well to choose this option if you have kids that might be constantly scratching the tank or tossing their toys in that direction. And since they're harder to scratch they're actually easier to clean. A plain razor blade can be used for algae and other materials that stick to the tank whereas acrylic tanks need much more careful attention.

In the end it's up to you to decide which is best for your home and your particular arrangement. And by the way, there's no credible truth to the rumor that acrylic is bad for the fish or in any way emits or releases chemicals in the water that is harmful. While some rumor mills like to continuously regurgitate these types of things, so far no one has found any credible evidence to support this claim. So if acrylic works best for you, then go for it!

Accessories

Obviously you can't just fill your tank with water and toss some fish in; not if you expect them to live through the night that is! Just like you need things to survive every day including food and oxygen, and need those utilities turned on before you can move into a new residence, your fish need the water at the right temperature and with the right chemicals before they can survive it. So let's go over the accessories you need for your tank and cover some of the details about each one; in a later section we'll go into detail about how to actually put everything together and get your tank ready for habitation.

The heater.

Have you ever stuck your toe into a body of water, whether it's a lake or pool, and thought that there was no way you're going into that frigid place? Even with our own natural insulation and production of body heat, we as humans are very sensitive to a cold environment and this includes cold bodies of water.

Now imagine if you're a tiny little fish with only a thin set of scales as insulation and a small amount of heat radiating from your body!

That cold water is literally a death sentence. So having a good heater in your tank is important, but you may have noticed that there is a wide variety of models and styles from which to choose. Why the differences, and which is best for your tank?

You'll note on most heaters that they will state the size of tank they're compatible with, and it's important to make sure you find this on the label and get the appropriate size. After that, you have your choices of submersible, hanging, or substrate heaters.

Submersible and hanging are just that - they either go in the water completely or hang from the tank, and the only real difference between them is aesthetics. The hanging heaters poke out behind your aquarium and some find this unsightly, whereas the submersible heaters are completely covered in your tank.

Substrate heaters are two coils that you cross at the bottom of your aquarium and then cover with gravel and other elements so that they are completely invisible. Most aquarium owners claim that these are the best for even heating of your tank, since other heaters of course will be warmer near the actual heating element.

Usually there's no need to pick substrate over any of the other models when it comes to even heating because both hanging and submersible heaters do the trick quite nicely and aren't so warm that they're dangerous to the fish.

Also, it's been reported that when you have a problem with a substrate heater you actually need to pull apart just about your entire tank since it's buried underneath everything. So other than how you want your heater to look, you only need to keep in mind the size of tank you have and your budget.

Lighting.

Light in an aquarium provides much more than just ambience; it's important for the health of the fish, plants, and even the water itself. A tank that's too brightly lit will get too hot and fish will die, whereas not enough light means the fish and vegetation will both wither up and die. Also, the entire reason you bring a tank into your home is to see the fish, right? If the lighting is too dim you won't get the full effect of the tank itself and if it's too bright it won't be pleasant to look at and may be a distraction.

Lighting may then sound a bit complicated but it really doesn't need to be. Only extremes of too much light or not enough are going to be very dangerous. Let's take a look at the different types of lights and bulbs that are going to be appropriate for your tank.

Florescent lighting is usually the first choice of all aquarium owners since it is a soft light, doesn't generate much heat, and uses only a minor amount of electricity. For smaller aquariums, many opt for compact florescent lights although these are a bit more expensive.

The most expensive lights are called metal halide, and while they are ideal for larger aquariums because of the amount of light they produce they are the most expensive of all choices. They are used only with open top aquariums because of the amount of heat they produce.

If you're not already aware, lights go over the top of the aquarium and need to be matched by the size of it. Make sure you find out the dimensions of your tank and only purchase lights that fit the width of the tank. Many tanks and tank kits come with lights already attached to them, but if you're buying a used tank or purchasing everything separately then you'll need to get just the right lighting for your tank.

The filter.

In lakes or oceans, nature acts as a natural filter for impurities and harmful agents that are in the water. This is why fish can swim in what is realistically their own bathroom and not get sick, since the water current keeps everything in motion and all the vegetation and other elements filter all these elements and help them to break down as well.

In your tank at home a filter is imperative for the health of your fish, vegetation, and overall condition of the tank.

Impurities will get trapped in the water and cling to the walls of your tank as well; this is not only unsightly but it's downright dangerous for the fish as well. Any experienced aquarium owner will tell you that the filter is the heart of the tank and the one area where you do not want to skimp when it comes to quality. Sure, you can get a low-cost filter but your fish will not be healthy, your tank will need cleaning more often, and you'll wind up paying more in replacement cartridges down the road. But when we say quality and mention low-cost, don't think that the most expensive filters are necessarily the best either. Here are some things to consider when it comes to filters:

Nature's own filter is the sponge; its unique design traps all sorts of elements and allows them to break down without being released in the ocean or body of water. To that end, sponge filters are the simples of aquarium filters but are very effective, despite the fact that they look so simple and even downright ugly!

Cleaning a sponge filter means squeezing it out into separate aquarium water (tap water kills the helpful bacteria and other agents in a sponge). Usually for tanks larger than 20 gallons you need multiple filters; you also need to be sure you position them correctly so that smaller fish don't get trapped underneath them.

Under gravel filters have quite a few advantages and disadvantages, so this option needs to be weighed carefully.

Some tank owners argue that they are the best filters there are, since they are very close to how natural biology is balanced in the real oceans and seas. The water gets pulled through the gravel on the bottom of the tank which is necessary for the right types of bacteria and nitrates and so that waste is broken down effectively, keeping the tank clean and healthy. However, this constant pulling of the water through the gravel also means that circulation in the tank slows down, which can throw those healthy balances out of control.

The key to having an under gravel filter is frequent gravel cleaning or vacuuming with a special tool, and by frequent we mean at least once per week. For some people this is more maintenance than they care for, but if you can dedicate yourself to this schedule then under gravel may be the way to go.

Internal and external power filters are small machines that do the filtering for you. As with all others they have their advantages and disadvantages; internal filters are more aesthetically pleasing since they are buried in the tank decorations so you can push your aquarium up against the wall and not see the filter itself. External filters hang on the outside of the tank so while they're a bit more unsightly they're easier to access so cleaning and replacing them is more convenient.

The most highly recommended of all models are canister filters.

They typically offer the best filtration especially for larger tanks and because they are an enclosed system they allow for stronger filtration than most other power filters. A tank can be placed closer to the wall than most external filters, but they are some of the most expensive filters on the market.

And there are what are known as wet/dry filters. For these types, one part of the filtration media is not fully submerged, so they provide the best filtration and balance of chemicals needed for a healthy environment. Usually these types of filters are kept under the tank and so they are out of sight, allowing the tank to be placed flush against the wall.

pH Testers

The pH of your water is going to be one of the best meters you can have to know whether or not the water needs to be treated in any way. Testing your water is very easy and takes only minutes; you can purchase more expensive kits that require you to take samples of the water and add drops of other chemicals, or you can purchase simple pH strips. These are available at any pet supply store and are very inexpensive; you need to check your water about once per week so a kit of 100 strips will last you almost two years.

Air Pumps

Should you get an air pump for your tank? Many people think that they need one for aerating their tank, but your filter typically does an adequate job of this. The main purpose of an air pump is for decoration; the bubbles and small pebbles and other objects that get moved around by an air pump just make the experience more enjoyable. If you want an air pump and can afford it, then by all means invest in one but it's typically not necessary if you have an adequate filtration system.

Putting It Together

So you have your tank, you have a heater, some lights and a filter. Plug everything in, fill it with water, and toss in some fish, right?

In reality it takes up to six weeks for your water to be treated properly before you can introduce fish and vegetation to your tank. It's very important that the water be ready for them. This includes adding nutrients to your tank, introducing vegetation, and making sure the pH is at a healthy level as well.

It's easy to be impatient with this process but think of it as more time you can use to shop around for just the right combination of fish you want to introduce to your tank!

Let's talk about how to prepare your tank properly and the additives you need before bringing in anything alive to your tank.

Preparing Your Tank, or Aquarium Cycling

Okay, so you probably know that you can't just fill your tank with tap water, turn on the heater and filter, and dump your fish in. There's an entire process needed to get the water into the right condition and with the right chemical balance before it's going to be habitable for your fish, and this is called aquarium cycling. Let's take a look at how to do this so that you can get those beautiful fish home where they belong!

Unpack and Clean Your Tank; Placement

Of course you want to start with a clean tank, but it's a common mistake of many first-time aquarium owners to clean the tank with soap or other cleansers, harsh abrasives, and so on. It is imperative that you use only warm water and a soft sponge or cloth to clean out the inside of it.

Even if you rinse the tank thoroughly you will always have a residue of anything you use as a cleanser inside and many of these chemicals are going to be harmful and deadly to your fish.

When you wash out your tank be sure to wipe it dry as well so that there is no residue of dust, dirt or anything else.

Remember that you need to have an electrical outlet nearby to plug in all your accessories; you can of course use an extension cord or surge strip, but you want your tank near an outlet so the cords can reach. If you're using an exterior heating or filter unit make sure there is room between the tank and the wall.

Whatever stand you use remember that your tank is going to weigh quite a bit once it's filled with water. Water weighs about 8.34 pounds per gallon, so for a fifty gallon tank, that's anywhere from 250 to 400 pounds (your tank won't be completely full and of course you'll have vegetation, rocks, and so on).
If you're not sure about your stand, get a different one just to be sure! Many aquariums come with their own stands but if you get one without, be sure you don't skimp on the stand for it.

Keep the aquarium out of direct sunlight as this will cause the water to get too warm.

Install Your Accessories

If you want a backdrop in your aquarium you add it before anything else. Then you install your heater according to the manufacturer's directions; remember that if you use an under gravel heater or cables you need to add these before gravel or anything else.

It's important to follow the manufacturer's instructions on how to install your accessories and get them started; each model of course is different in how the tubes and such are attached and how to get them going.

Substrate.

Substrate refers to materials at the bottom of an aquarium. You can purchase sand or gravel made especially for tanks but it's important to prepare it as well for the tank. There is usually quite a bit of debris and other elements in these things, even when store-bought, so you need to rinse these before adding them. Place them in a bucket of regular tap water, stir everything with a stick or wooden spoon, then empty the water from the bucket and add some fresh water; repeat this until the water you add is completely clear. Make sure you just use plain water, as any type of cleanser is going to contaminate the tank.

Adding nutrients.

For vegetation and fish, you want to add nutrients to this environment but you don't simply dump these things in the water the way you might think. It's important to add nutrients over the top of the substrate after this has been added but before you add water. Usually just any type of general nutrients or what is called micronutrients are sufficient for your tank; add the amount directed on the package according to the size of your tank.

Preparing the rocks and wood.

Would you believe that not all rocks are appropriate for an aquarium? Or that wood needs some special treatment before it should be added as well?
It's surprising how many beginners just grab virtually anything they have in their own yard and toss it into an aquarium, and then wonder why their fish are sick and their water is cloudy.

Not all rocks are chemically suitable for aquariums. You can purchase rocks that are from your pet supply store, or a quick home test is to put your rocks in a bucket and pour some vinegar over them. If they fizz then they're not suitable for your tank as they contain harmful chemicals.

For those rocks that are appropriate and pass your home test, but that you haven't purchased from the store, be sure you rinse them thoroughly, spread them on a towel and use a wire brush to clean them before adding them.

As for the wood you want to add to your aquarium, even driftwood can have chemicals called tannins that get steeped like tea and that turn your water brown. They're not necessarily dangerous but they are very unsightly. To avoid this, take the wood you want to add and put it in a bucket of water; completely submerge it, adding a rock or something else on top to keep it under water if necessary. Let it soak for at least two days and you'll probably notice the water has turned brown. Drain the water and refill the bucket, letting it sit again for another two days. Repeat this until the water remains clear.

Preparing wood for your aquarium may take anywhere from one to two weeks, so don't rush this process.

Remember that you should only ever add driftwood to your aquarium and not wood that you pick up from the front yard or anywhere else. Regular wood can easily rot in water and kill your fish, not to mention that it contaminates the entire environment.

Vegetation

You need to introduce your vegetation before adding water of course; it's very hard to plant vegetation under water!

Adding vegetation to your substrate is a lot like adding plants to a garden. You need to be very careful of the roots of the plants and gently work them into the gravel or underneath the rocks. It's also helpful to plan out your vegetation just like you would an actual garden. It's very easy to just start purchasing plants that look good and then to find out that you have too much for your tank, or that you don't have enough and your tank looks somewhat bare.

Plant from left to right and from back to front. It's more visually appealing for larger and fuller plants to be in the back and one corner. You plant your vegetation in the tank just like you do the garden - scoop out enough from the substrate, place your plant in that hole, and close it up. Be sure you leave enough room between your plants so that they all have adequate room for their own roots.

Some people allow themselves to get very overwhelmed when it comes to the vegetation in their aquarium, wanting guidance on how to make the "right" decision and choices. But the vegetation you add to your aquarium is just like the flowers you plant in your garden - simply choose the ones that appeal to you personally, and make sure you keep in mind the space you have and your budget as well. You might need to play around with the planting a few times, moving a few things around or adding and taking away some items. But there is no right or wrong way to add vegetation to your aquarium, just like there's no right or wrong flowers to add to your garden. Do what looks best to you and you're sure to have success.

Adding the Water

It's very important that you add water in the proper manner when filling your aquarium. This means not just dumping it in with a pitcher, as this would scatter your substrate and other elements from the impact. Instead, place a sturdy plate in the middle of your aquarium and add water to the top of this very gently; you'll notice the water spills over the side of the plate slowly and fills your tank with the smallest amount of disturbance to your substrate.

You want to fill your tank only about 3/4 of the way full. This will allow for your plants to grow and to allow air to circulate properly in and around the tank.

It's important to add some tap water conditioner to the water at this point; conditioner will help to get chlorine and other additives out of the water so that your fish will be healthy. When you purchase tap water additive you add as much as directed on the label.

Add and Test the Chemicals

Water that is going to sustain fish is going to need elements that aren't found in tap water, and this includes healthy bacteria, nitrates, and elements like this. These things aren't going to grow on their own, so you need to add some things that are going to spur their growth.

Growing bacteria.

We often think of bacteria as being harmful and it's true that some are, but they also provide a valuable function in all processes of life as they keep the levels of other chemicals even and steady. This includes ammonia and nitrate, two chemicals produced by fish themselves because of their waste and feeding. Without good bacteria these levels of ammonia and nitrates become harmful and your fish die. So you need to get some good healthy bacteria growing in your water before you toss in any fish.

The products to look for are called cycle starters, and they include Bio-Spira, Stability, and Septo-Bac. You simply add one of these according to the label directions for your tank size. It takes sometimes a good two weeks or even longer to grow a healthy environment for your fish so give this plenty of time.

Test the chemicals.

How do you know when it's time to add some fish? It's simple - you purchase an expensive chemical test kit from your pet supply store and test the water. It's that simple.

If you notice that your water is still not ready after two weeks, you can easily drop a few bits of flake food in the water to get the reaction going.

Your First Fish

Adding your first fish is the last part of aquarium cycling, as the fish themselves are an important part of having water that is capable of supporting them.

But again, running out and just dumping in all the fish you want is not wise at this point and is a common mistake of many beginners. It's recommended that instead you start with just one fish of a very hearty variety. A Zebra Danio or Black Widow Tetra are both good suggestions for a cycling fish. Allow just one of two of these to stay in the water alone for another two weeks while monitoring the chemical levels before you add any more.

Water Changes

When you add even one fish you'll notice on your water testing that the ammonia and nitrate levels go up; this is natural and healthy. Note what your chemical test kit says about a tank of your size and monitor these levels carefully.

If your ammonia or nitrite levels start to reach a harmful level, you need to do a water change. This means emptying and adding fresh water, but only about 25%-50% of what is in your tank depending on how high these chemicals reach. Most find that they need to do this about once per week for a good four weeks into your aquarium cycling.

It's usually after about six weeks that you notice the chemicals are staying at a healthy range with minimal water changes. It's at this time that you can then start adding additional fish!

Let's look at the varieties of fish that are readily available to you so you can start thinking about what you may want to add, and how many of each.

Varieties of Tropical Fish

So you're ready to add some additional fish to your aquarium; congratulations! But as strange as it may sound, it's best to find out something about the many varieties of fish out there before you start shopping since fish can often act like other animals when it comes to aggression, territory, and so on.

Most people don't realize this; they think that fish are just fish and all they do all day is swim around aimlessly. In reality fish have behavior characteristics much like other animals, so let's take a closer look at some of these so you can make an informed decision before you plunk down your hard-earned money on a variety or breed that's going to cause you some problems.

Remember, plan your tank the way you would plan anything else - carefully and with some thought!

The auratus is an aggressive fish and intolerant of others in its territory. The auratus likes rocks and caves and so should have plenty in any home aquarium. You should only have these in larger aquariums so they have plenty of space away from other fish.

There are many varieties of angelfish, from albino to koi, black, blushing, golden, and many others. While they do survive with flake food alone, angelfish do much better with some live food from time to time so only purchase them if you can invest in live food.

The blue acara are very beautiful, very hardy, and typically mesh well with all other fish in the tank. They are a popular choice for aquarium enthusiasts.

The cockatoo dwarf cichlid are very rare fish and somewhat difficult to find but usually thrive quite easily and add a nice burst of color to your collection.

The convict cichlid are called the barroom brawlers of aquariums because they are very aggressive and can hold their own against other fish. Be careful of adding these to your tank! They are interesting to watch but should be kept in larger tanks only.

The discus cichlid are very rare and very difficult to maintain because they are so sensitive to their environment. It's not usually recommended that beginners try to maintain these fish in their tanks.

The black molly is one of the most common forms of fish found in aquariums. Because of breeding techniques they are also available in a wide variety of other colors and sizes. They are typically very sturdy and do well in most home tanks.

The guppy is the most common of all tropical fish found in home aquariums. This is because they are hearty, easy to raise, and very colorful.

Swordfish are also one of the most popular of all tank fish, as they are easy to maintain, very hardy, and seem to get along well with so many other types of fish. They may not be the most eye-catching but they are good "filler" fish for any tank.

American flag fish are somewhat rare but still favorites of many tank owners since they are tolerant of a wide variety of water conditions. They have a beautiful look and get along well with other fish.

The neon tetra is a favorite of most hobbyists because of their unique coloring and brightness. They are a bit finicky about their environment but can do well in an established tank that is well maintained.

Like their neon cousins, the glowlight tetra is not that common with tank owners but are very interesting to look at. They too can be a bit finicky but will thrive in a tank that is kept properly and seem to get along with other fish.

The black-finned pacu are often mistaken for piranha, and those who own them love their large size and dominance. However, they can grow to over a foot in length so they're only for larger tanks! The one at right is an amazing 17 inches in length.

The banded leporinus is a favorite among tank owners because of its striped appearance but a very difficult fish to keep. They nip, fight other fish, and are good jumpers so you need large tank with enough room for other fish to avoid it and that can be kept tightly sealed.

The electric yellow labidochromis is a favorite for hobbyists, obviously for its striking color. It also has a great temperament and gets along well with other fish, making it a mainstay of most tank owners.

The festivum is a great addition to any tank since it is very hearty and gets along with most other fish. It's a great addition to any tank and nicely complements virtually any other fish.

The flower horn fish are one of those fish that you either love or hate. It is a very hardy fish and does well in all sorts of environments. They do grow to be quite large so they are best in only the largest of aquariums.

The frontosa fish are very easy to breed, thrive in most environments, and are generally of good temperaments.

The giraffe cichlid is very popular not just for its color but because it's a hearty fish that gets along well with other fish. They do grow to a good ten inches so of course they're best in larger aquariums but are very enjoyable to keep.

The Jack Dempsey fish have been around forever when it comes to home tanks but they are very territorial and finicky around other fish. They are good only in the largest of aquariums where they have room to be away from other species.

The keyhole cichlid are very peaceful fish and make a great addition to any tank. They are general tolerant of their environment and are a favorite of most tank owners.

The rainbow cichlid provide a great burst of color when needed and are more temperament than many other fish.

The ram cichlid is a very peaceful fish but does not do well with more aggressive species and varieties. While they are beautiful to look at they need to be kept away from predators.

The black neon are also very easy fish to raise and maintain, and against a dark background or substrate they are very interesting to look at.

Sometimes mistaken for goldfish but with a much deeper color, the serpae tetra are easy fish to maintain and are very calm, getting along well with other fish. They provide a great contrast to darker fish in your tank.

The silver hatchet fish are very interesting because sometimes they are very active and sometimes they are virtually motionless, but they are an interesting variety that seem to get along well with other species.

Barbs come in a few different varieties and are rare and expensive. They are a great addition to any tank but because of their cost should be introduced sparingly and only if you are very conscientious about their environment.

Betta splendens are often found by themselves in small bowls but they do much better in larger environments. They are a great addition to virtually any tank and get along with most other species.

Gouramis come in a wide variety such as the honey, pictured here. They are typically shy and docile and wouldn't do well with overly aggressive fish, but otherwise make a great addition to any tank.

Choosing Your Fish

There are obviously dozens more varieties of tropical fish you could add to your own collection; this is only meant as an introduction to the most popular varieties and what you need to consider when adding any to your own tank.

Fish are like all other animals; they have their own personality, temperament, and interact differently with other fish as well. It's very important when choosing any varieties that you consider not just how they look but how well they'll do in your size tank, the other species you already have, and whether or not you feel capable of minding your tank enough for the more sensitive varieties.

This is also very important to remember if you ever plan on breeding your fish, which we'll discuss in a later section. Fish need optimal conditions and environment when they breed and having other fish that are overly aggressive or predatory will interrupt this process and may keep it from happening altogether. Remember, your fish are living creatures and not just objects and they rely on you to provide them with a happy and healthy environment.

Do your homework and add fish slowly, and you'll no doubt find a great mix that everyone in your home enjoys.

Common Tank Problems

Even with the best of care and maintenance, tropical fish tanks are going to encounter problems. This is just part of the fact that fish and their environment are not exact sciences; it's best to be prepared for common tank problems and be ready to address them than it is to assume that you'll just maintain it regularly and nothing will go wrong.

Let's take a look at some common problems with tanks and see what we can do to fix them.

Green Water

While green water may happen in nature it's not pleasant for anyone, including fish. Green water in your tank is most likely caused by a buildup of algae, so figuring out why you have an excessive amount of algae is the key to fixing this problem.

Overfeeding.

When fish food breaks down it contributes to an algae problem. If you still have any number of flakes left over a good ten minutes or so after feeding your fish, you may be overfeeding. You of course don't want to go overboard in the other direction and start underfeeding your fish, so just cut back a little bit at the next feeding and see if they eat all that. If not, cut back just a little bit more. Keep track of how much you give them until you reach the amount that they eat entirely with only a few flakes left over. That's going to be the right amount.

Water changes.

Changing out the water is a tedious chore but it's a necessary one as well. Algae thrive in dirty water. A water change should be done once per week; larger tanks only need about 10% of their water changed out since the larger environment helps keep the water cleaner whereas moderate and smaller tanks need 25%-35% of the water changed.

To change your water you need to use what is called an aquarium vacuum, small little hoses with a sort of pump attached to them. You run this over the gravel and along the plants as these areas collect the most algae and other harmful materials. The hose empties out the water into a bucket, and you then slowly replace the water in your tank.

It's important to adjust your heater when you do water changes so that it's warm enough for the sensitive fish, and then readjust it again once it's reached optimal temperature.

Too much light.

Algae thrive in light, so you may need to move your aquarium away from a window and adjust the lighting fixture itself to a dimmer wattage. It's important to turn the lights off at night, just as you would any other light.

Chemical treatments.

There are chemical treatments you can use for algae buildup but these should be used as a last resort. Any chemical you introduce to your tank is going to affect your fish, so it's good to try other changes first before turning to chemical treatments.

Cloudy or White Water

Cloudy water usually signals a bacteria buildup and there are a few common causes for this. Usually if you have not properly cleaned your decorations or substrate, this causes cloudiness.

Remember that these need to be prepared for your tank before putting them inside, unless you've purchased them in a prepared state. Even then, it's best to do the soaking process for all your aquarium decorations and accessories just to be sure.

Sometimes when you give your fish medication, have just set up your tank, or have just cleaned it the bacteria levels can spike causing the water to be white or cloudy. Usually you don't need to do much in these cases except wait for the situation to clear up on its own. Using chemicals should also be a last resort in these cases and only if you have waited a few days to see if the water would clear up on its own.

High or Low pH

Most tropical fish need a pH level between 6.5 and 7.5. When you test your water's pH you'll get a reading as to where you're at and may need to make adjustments accordingly. Most varieties of fish have no problem with the small fluctuations between 6.5 and 7.5, but some of the more finicky species may need more monitoring and adjustments. If you pH falls outside these levels you need to make some changes as well.

Raising the pH.

The higher your pH, the less acid you have in the tank. A quick way to get some acidic elements out is to do a water change. Usually if you a water change and then give the water a few days, the acid will adjust itself. Bacteria and other elements will get adjusted which will in turn adjust the pH.

If you do a water change and still have very low pH after a few days, it's time to consider chemical treatments.

Lowering the pH.

When you need to lower the pH it's always recommended that you try some natural remedies and methods first as many chemical treatments for lowering pH encourage algae growth, which is just as bad for the fish and the tank as a high acid level.
Try adding some additional driftwood or peat to your tank to lower the pH. Crushed coral raises a tank's pH, so remove some of this from your tank; you can also remove some substrate.

If you must use chemicals to lower your tank's pH, use them sparingly and cautiously. Try the minimum amount recommended on their label and re-test your pH after a few days.

Water Hardness

If you have hard water at home you may see residue of calcium buildup on the shower heads and sinks. Your skin and hair may also be very dry.

Water hardness means that you have a high level of calcium carbonate in the water; this happens with tap water as well as with water in your tank. Hard water doesn't really hurt your fish that much but you should check it at least once per month to be sure that it isn't getting out of hand, since water hardness can affect the pH level as well.

You can purchase water hardness testing kits at your supply store which will tell you how to understand the reading. If you have a problem with hard water you can purchase a very inexpensive water hardness "pillow" that you add to your tank, or you can filter the water through peat moss as well. If it's not hard enough you can add a small amount of baking soda.

These are just a few of the more common problems that you may experience with a tropical fish tank. If you notice problem with the equipment or accessories, you need to speak to the store where you purchased them or they may need to be replaced. Check all your equipment at least monthly for problems with the heater, filter, and so on, and be sure you're following the recommended guidelines for each. If your filter model recommends a certain changing schedule, follow it.

Common Problems with Your Fish

You may run into a problem with your fish that is unique to that individual fish but there are some common health problems or behavioral problems that tropical fish have which you may need to address. Let's take a look at them in greater detail here so you can be aware of them and can correct them as well.

Fish Ick or Ich

Yes, that's a real name for a condition your fish may get. It is characterized by white drops or spots on their body and that they are suddenly getting slow or sluggish.

Fish ick/ich is really an organism that starts in the water and that attaches itself to your fish where it stays for a while before letting go so that it can float free again.

Fish ick/ich has a particular cycle of about three weeks, so you may notice your fish with the condition for only a short time.

To combat this problem before it really affects your fish, raise the water temperature to about eighty degrees so that it's too warm for the fish ick/ich to survive on your fish. They release, and then you can add a small amount of medication to the water to get rid of them completely. It's a good idea to continue adding medication for a full two weeks to be sure it's gone entirely.

Fish ick/ich is rather common in many tanks and is not typically a sign of anything more serious that's wrong with your fish or your tank, but it's a condition that should still be address promptly.

Dropsy

Dropsy eats away at your fish's internal organs. It is a very dangerous disease and one that can kill your fish easily if not taken care of. While there are many things you can do to treat the disease, it's always better to prevent it in the first place.

The symptoms of dropsy are difficult to detect except for the trained eye. Your fish needs to be very sick on the inside to show signs on the outside. A swollen abdomen and scales that stick out slightly are the most common symptoms of dropsy. Listlessness, not eating properly, a change in color, or spending more time at the top of bottom of the tank are also common symptoms of stress, so these too might be present when any fish is sick.

Dropsy is not a contagious disease so you don't need to notice symptoms on more than one fish for it to be present. However it is possible for one fish to pass it on to another so a sick fish should be put in a quarantine tank if you suspect dropsy.

Antibiotics are best for treating dropsy, as well as adding a teaspoon of aquarium salt per ten gallons of water to your tank to kill the bacteria that may be present.

The most common cause of dropsy is poor water quality. Changing you water on a regular basis cannot be emphasized enough when it comes to your tank's condition and the health of your fish overall.

If you change your water and use antibiotics and still don't notice any change in your sick fish, it's time to seek medical help. Dropsy is very serious and will cost you the fish's life, as well as other fish if not caught in time, so it needs to be addressed.

Fin Rot

Who would have thought that something that lives in the water could actually get any type of rot?

In reality fin rot is a very common condition for many tropical fish, but it is also a very treatable condition.

Rotted or ragged looking fins, white edges on fins, or puffy sores on the fins, are all signs of fin rot. In the later stages of fin rot you might also notice a loss of appetite.

Typically it's a buildup of bacteria that causes fin rot, so again, water changing is imperative to keep your fish healthy. Stress is also a factor, and the thing that gives fish the most stress is bad water quality. You must change your water and have regular testing and corrections when needed. Remember, your fish are relying on you to make up for the fact that they don't live in nature with its natural filters and cleansers.

Bullies are another cause of fin rot; more aggressive species of fish may nip at other fish, making their fins more susceptible to injury and disease. Be careful about your selection of fish when stocking your tank and make sure that if you must have aggressive fish that your tank is large enough so that there can be separation between them and other fish.

If improving your water quality does not help the fin rot, there are antibiotics you can purchase which help. Make sure you're doing everything you can to correct the conditions that bring on fin rot as you use the course of medication as well, since if you don't you'll just have more cases.

Preventing Common Diseases

An ounce of prevention is definitely worth a pound of cure, especially when talking about your very valuable tropical fish. Since they are in a contained environment there are very few reasons why they should get sick or infected if you the owner are doing everything you can to keep them in a healthy environment. Let's cover some of these important parts here.

Beware of overfeeding.

Food flakes that are not eaten float in the water where they break down and release bacteria and other harmful elements. If you notice after five or ten minutes of feeding your fish that there are still a good number of flakes in the water (a few flakes are normal) then you're probably overfeeding.

If you suspect that you are, cut back only a small amount and very slowly. You don't want to underfeed your fish either, so reduce the amount in very small increments until you have only a few flakes left after feeding.

Cleaning the tank.

Doing a change of water, vacuuming your substrate and cleaning the tank's walls will go a long way toward keeping the environment healthy for your fish. This also includes doing weekly testing for pH and other chemicals and making adjustments as necessary. Keep the water at a healthy temperature and make sure your filter is working properly, and is cleaned or rinsed as often as recommended. Skimping on any of these things is a surefire way to have sick fish, so resist the temptation to cut corners in these areas.

Of course you don't want to overdo it either. Your water needs certain forms of bacteria to be healthy, so don't think you need to do a water change every day. Just be thorough every week and you'll be fine.

Beware of bullies.

Some of the more aggressive fish will attack some of the more shy fish and cause physical harm, which may or may not be terribly damaging but certainly leaves them more vulnerable to illnesses and disease.

It's so important to be educated about your fish and the common behavior problems with some species and to make sure you're not including overly aggressive fish in your tank, especially if it's only a medium or small size. Keep an eye on these fish and observe their behavior; if any seem overly aggressive, consider removing them from the tank.

Taking Care of Your Fish

Avoiding disease and sickness is of course important when it comes to caring for your fish but so is taking care of them every single day. It's important to know how and when to feed them, what they need for breeding, and so on.

Feeding

You may see on the back of fish food labels the warning not to overfeed your fish, and you would think that if anyone would want you to give too much food to your fish it would be those selling the product - so if they're warning against it, then it must be important!

Remember that in their natural habitat fish don't eat every few hours the way humans do; typically they even go a day or two without food and are perfectly fine. They eat when they can find food and store food for those times when they can't.

If you're feeding your fish a moderate amount twice per day then you're probably giving them plenty. A few flakes left over after feeding is fine, but too many will break down in the tank and cause a buildup of bacteria and other harmful elements.

When you approach your tank you may notice that the fish head for the top as if ready to feed. This shouldn't be taken as a sign that they are actually hungry or need food; often they simply do this as an instinctive response and not truly as a sign that they need or even want food. Give them a modest amount twice per day and your fish will be fine. They will expect food at regular times so try to do this on a regular schedule; if you feed them before you go to work during the week, then feed them as early as possible on the weekends so that it's at least close to when they get food on other days.

Types of Food

For most house pets you have two types of food - wet and dry. With tropical fish, who knew there could be so many types and varieties? There are some things to think about when deciding what type is best for the fish you have and their health overall. As with other pets and animals, there are some foods that are used as staples and some that should be considered treats.

Fish food flakes.

The mainstay of any fish's diet and the most popular staple you can purchase for your fish as well. They are cheap and available virtually anywhere, and have virtually everything your fish need by way of vitamins, minerals, and other nutrients. If you have a species tank you can easily find flakes geared toward that particular species or generic flakes that do well for all varieties of tropical fish.

Fish food pellets.

The one major difference between flakes and pellets is that pellets sink to the ground much quicker. Some fish have a preference for one over the other; if your fish seem finicky with flakes you may want to try pellets to see if that will do the trick. Remember that in their natural habitat some fish get their food from the ground so they just naturally gravitate toward the bottom of the tank when it's feeding time.

Live Fish Food

Ewww. Yes, live fish food is exactly what it sounds like, and includes brine shrimp, bloodworms, earthworms, and feeder fish.

Some fish are carnivorous and prefer some type of meat in their diet, however, these types of live fish food are not typically to be considered staples but as a delicacy or treat. They usually lack the same nutritional value as flakes or pellets and so should not be considered a main part of any fish's diet.

Freeze dried.

Not all live fish food is actually sold like bait, that is, alive and squirming. Other fish owners would be just as repulsed as you probably are. Instead many are freeze dried which makes them not only more palatable for you to deal with but greatly increases their shelf life as well. Freeze dried fish food is rather expensive so it does need to be used sparingly.

Frozen fish food.

Some of these types of live fish food are also available frozen. Most are divided up by species of fish so if you have a species tank then you can search for these as well. Because they're frozen their shelf life is also quite a bit longer than other forms of live fish food.

Brine shrimp.

Brine shrimp are considered the most popular of all live fish food but are expensive as well. They are a favorite for baby fish because of their size. It is actually possible to breed your own brine shrimp if you're very determined and enthusiastic about this hobby. Otherwise they are available live, frozen or freeze dried.

Blood worms.

Ewww again. Bloodworms are a favorite treat of carnivorous fish but should be considered as a treat and not a staple of their diet. Just as worms are used for bait when out fishing on the lake, fish love the taste of worms and are attracted to their scent very easily. Feel free to say ewww yet again.

Breeding

So you want to get more fish? Run out and buy them, or let nature take its course and allow your fish to make new ones!

Fish breeding is one of the most natural occurrences in the world and happens much easier than with just about any other animal. While it's a good idea to get other pets spayed or neutered, allowing your fish to breed can be an exciting process.

It's important to remember that as with other animals there's not much you need to do to have your fish breed. As long as they are comfortable in their environment and have access to one another, breeding is almost assured to happen.

There are some things that you should think about however since your fish are in an unnatural environment and so may need some adjustments made for a healthy breeding experience.

Quarantine tank.

Putting your fish in a quarantine tank may be a good idea for breeding; this is simply a smaller version of your fish tank set aside for any fish that need to be separated. Sometimes a sick fish will need to be put in a quarantine tank but if you have mixed species or more aggressive fish in your large tank, it's a good idea to put your breeders in the quarantine tank. This is for their protection while they breed, the protection of the female when she's pregnant, and protection for the eggs and fry (baby fish).

Mind the water conditions.

The water in your tank must be optimal for breeding to happen. Anything that's off and a fish will instinctively hold off breeding, assuming that their babies will be in danger. It's only when their habitat is virtually perfect and safe will they feel it okay to start mating. Make sure you keep the water at the right temperature and chemical balance for this particular breed; make corrections as necessary.
Make sure your fish are "compatible."

It is very easy with some breeds to have a difficult time telling the males from the females. A common mistake with many newcomers and hobbyists is to assume that as long as there are two fish they'll breed, not realizing that they have two males or two females. An experienced fish expert at your pet supply store can tell for you or give you more specific examples of what to look for when it comes to males and females, and of course you can look up online for this particular breed. You may also want to have more than one pair in the quarantine tank just in case one is getting older or is sick and you don't realize it; fish that are not in optimal health will not breed and may be rejected by potential mates as well.

Give them privacy.

Okay, it's not that your breeding fish actually need privacy because they're embarrassed to do the deed in front of you but most breeding fish like places to hide because it keeps them safe from predators.

Bear in mind that in their natural habitat, a fish that is breeding, that is pregnant, eggs and baby fish are all much more susceptible to predators because of their weakened physical state. Be sure you have plenty of plants, rocks, or a nice castle for them to hide behind.

Try target or dither fish.

A target fish is one that is a bit more aggressive than the species you're trying to breed; the idea is that the pair you want to breed join forces against the target fish when placed in the quarantine tank with them. This makes them feel more like a couple and more attached to one another so that they're more likely to be comfortable breeding.

A dither fish is just the opposite; it's a very calming and soothing fish meant to help other fish realize things are safe. Some fish are very temperamental and somewhat shy or easily agitated and hide or avoid fish even of their own species. A dither fish is meant to swim around slowly in a calming way and thus reassures the shy fish that everything is safe, thereby coaxing him or her out of hiding.

For target or dither fish, this will depend on the species you are trying to breed. Make sure your target fish isn't overly aggressive or predatory, and remember that you only want one added to the quarantine tank. Also, give your intended breeding fish some time to try things on their own before introducing these other fish as it may just take a few days for them to get things going.

Give them some treats.

Just like humans, some nice delicacies can relax a fish and make him or her more in the mood for breeding.

Try giving your fish some live food, either fresh or frozen, that may be pleasing to them. If their bellies are full then they may relax and feel more in the mood for reproducing.

Make it rain.

Most fish breed during the rainy season, for whatever reason. It may relax them or it may mean extra cover for privacy and protection.

To reproduce this atmosphere in your home tank, try 5%-10% water changes every day or every other day with water that is just slightly cooler than your tank water. This may simulate the rainy condition and the slight change in temperature may also help to relax but invigorate the fish as well.

Of course even with all these steps there is no guarantee that your fish will mate and that it will lead to a successful offspring, and if you've done all you can and still no babies it may be time to try with another pair. Sometimes fish are older than you think or not in the best of health, or for another reason just aren't going to mate. You can't actually force this so it's best to just try another species or couple.

Taking Care of Your Tank

You need to care for your tank on an everyday basis in order for your fish to be happy and healthy. This means not just knowing the things you should do but also the things you should avoid doing as well. Let's take a look at how you can care for your tank every single day.

Mind Your Cleansers

Do you honestly think that bleach is present in a fish's natural habitat? Of course not. And yet it's surprising how many people think that they should use that on their tank when they want to get it really, really clean.

Bleach almost always leaves a residue or some of the substance behind, no matter how much you rinse the tank or wipe it down after using it. When you clean your tank, use just plain water. For stubborn algae you can use a razorblade or clean putty knife or other straight edge to scrape it, but you don't need to use harsh cleansers on this either.

Remember that in the oceans where tropical fish live it's never in an antiseptic state. Some bacteria are good for the fish, and water that is overly cleaned or sanitized is not. While you want to keep a clean tank with clear water, you don't want to go overboard and strangle your fish with cleansers either.

Leave the Gravel Alone

Some hobbyists feel that they need to clean and sanitize the gravel as well, and are prone to taking it all out of the tank and rinsing it thoroughly before putting it back. Wrong! Your gravel does capture all the aquarium waste not filtered out but it also provides that balance of good bacteria levels as well. Rinsing it throws your entire chemical balance completely off and is very bad for your fish.

To properly clean your gravel use an aquarium vacuum and do a light cleaning once per week. This will pull up waste and other harmful materials while leaving the good stuff behind. It will also provide the least amount of disturbance to your fish while the tank is being cleaned.

Don't Clean Everything at Once

Again, in nature tropical fish aren't swimming in a sanitized environment and will always face some bacteria, germs, and so on. It's a common mistake for tank owners to think that when they clean the tank, this means everything. In reality if you do that overly thorough type of cleaning of all the elements in your tank at once, it's going to throw that chemical balance off as well.

It's recommended instead that you clean your tank in stages. One week do a water change and clean the glass, and the next week, clean the gravel, decorations, and so on. You can do a partial (10%-15%) water change on this alternative week to keep it clear and healthy.

We cannot emphasize it enough - you want to keep your tank clean but you don't want it so clean that it's unnatural for your fish.

Scrape the Walls

If you can't use bleach on the walls of your tank, how do you get them clean? By scraping of course.

This isn't anyone's idea of a fun job but it needs to be done regularly. If you have an acrylic tank you'll need to use a special tool made just for this medium as otherwise it will scratch and get ruined. For glass tanks you can use a razor or other straight edge. There are also scrubbing pads you can use that you get at your pet supply store, or a plain wet rag can get some of the slimy stuff off as well. But again, avoid using bleach or other cleansers under any circumstances.

It's best to leave some stuff behind when scraping the walls rather than being overly zealous when scraping.

Clean the Decorations

Even if you can't see a slimy film on your decorations they will still need to be cleaned regularly so that they don't get a nasty build-up of algae and other materials. Once very week or every other week you need to pull them out of the tank and give them a good rub down. This means all the corners and crevices as well. Again, a plain wet cloth is best; you need to avoid using cleansers on these just like you do the tank walls.

This means your larger rocks, castles, and plastic plants you may have. If you neglect doing this on a regular basis that algae will build up to the point where it's going to be very nasty to clean, so it's better to take care of it regularly while it's still manageable than to wait.

Clean the Filter

Another common mistake that many hobbyists make is to clean their filter out in tap water or a cleansing agent. It's usually best to just rinse your filter right in your tank's water so that you're not upsetting the chemical balance or mix of bacteria that's so important for your fish.

You can use a small brush or old toothbrush (please, not your roommate's or spouse's toothbrush!) to clean the mechanical parts and anything that may be stuck in the filter. Under gravel filters typically need to be left alone as the vacuuming you do on a regular basis will clean those.

Vacuum or Siphon the Substrate

This too needs to be done on a regular basis. When you vacuum the substrate you usually need a "catch" bucket to catch the dirty water. Remember that you want to do a good job but your gravel is not going to be perfectly cleaned at any one time.

When you use a vacuum or siphon you're going to be pulling water out of your tank and it's important to never remove more than 25%-35% of your water at any one time, whether it's because of vacuuming or water changes. After vacuuming replace the water you've pulled out with water of the same approximate temperature.

Do a Water Change

This needs to be done weekly or every other week at the most. The smaller your tank the more frequently it needs to be done and the more water you need to change out since smaller tanks have a harder time keeping themselves clean. Larger tanks are filtering their own water so you can go a bit longer and take out less water in the large tanks.

A good amount is about 15% of your water, or up to 25% for smaller tanks. Be sure you replace the water with water of the same temperature and add a tap water conditioner to your tank after you put in fresh water.

If you do all these things on a regular basis without going overboard, you're sure to have a tank that is clean enough for your fish without having harsh or damaging chemicals in your water.

Tropical Fish That Survive and Thrive - Or, Summing it All Up

Okay, "summing it all up" probably isn't the most grammatically correct phrase we could find, but you get the picture. Sometimes it's best to get the executive summary for a subject so that you can have a quick review or plan on what you want to do. Let's cover the most important points of introducing fish to your home and of keeping them happy and healthy.

Get a Big Tank, or Plan Accordingly

Fish need room to live and to thrive; those small little bowls you see for single goldfish really aren't the most ideal living conditions for them. It's like you trying to live out of your car. Sure it can be done, but who would enjoy that? Fish enjoy lots of space the same way that humans enjoy some elbow room.

So get the largest tank you can afford and fit into your home. If you can't get a huge tank, then you may need to adjust your plans accordingly. This means having less in your tank - less fish, less plants, less decorations.

Tropical fish can do quite well in tanks that are smaller but not if they're cramped or crowded. They need room to swim and explore their environment, and overcrowding your tank is going to make your fish feel as if they have a ton of roommates - cramped, crowded, nervous and edgy.

And of course the size of your tank brings us to the next point:

Plan Your Fish Carefully

Extremely large aquariums can support extremely large fish, or those that are bullies to other fish since there is room enough for them to keep to themselves. But if you have a smaller aquarium and put in some aggressive fish, you're going to have problems.

Also, some fish are very shy and docile and if you put them in with bully fish, they're going to get picked on no matter what. This isn't going to be healthy for them or the overall environment of the tank.

Most people get fish because they look so beautiful, but bear in mind that because a more aggressive fish looks beautiful doesn't mean it belongs in your tank. Having a fish that's too large for your tank is not kind and could be considered downright cruel, as they need to have room to swim for their physical and emotional health.

Having fish is just like having any other pet - it's a responsibility that you shouldn't take lightly. Keeping a large dog cooped up in a small apartment is very unkind to the dog, no matter how much the owners may deny it. In the same way, having overly aggressive fish in a tank with shy and docile fish that don't defend themselves or having fish that are really too large for your tank is not kind at all. Put some thought into your fish the same way you would plan any other investment or anything else you bring into your home; in the long run you'll be much happier if you do.

Be Patient during the Aquarium Cycling

When you get a new dog or cat you probably don't need to do much to bring him or her home. Get a few toys, blanket, and some food, fill a litter box for the cat and buy a leash for the dog, and you're pretty much good to go.

With fish it can be very difficult for the new hobbyist to wait those needed weeks for their water to be ready for them. It's a common mistake for some to dump in too many chemicals thinking that this will speed up the process or to bring fish home and add them before the water is ready.

Think of your aquarium cycling as being like baking a cake. Turning the oven up to 750 degrees isn't going to let it cook in half the time, and neither is doubling up on the baking soda you add. And if you pull it from the oven before it's fully cooked, what do you have but a big mess?

You can't rush baking just like you can't rush aquarium cycling. You need to be patient and let the water prepare itself, and adding fish before it's ready is like taking that cake out of the oven before it's done. You've ruined the process and can't do much to fix it.

So be patient. Your fish will come home soon enough, and in the long run you'll be glad you waited.

Make a Schedule for Cleaning and Stick to it

Cleaning your fish tank is like cleaning your own home - it needs to be done and on a regular basis. You probably wouldn't like eating from dirty dishes and having to use a nasty bathroom, and your fish won't like it either.

You don't want to clean too much either, so that's why a regular schedule is a good idea. It keeps your tank clean but not so clean that the chemical balance is off.

Using the right materials and the right techniques is important when cleaning your tank so that it's healthy and just clean enough for your fish, but not sanitized and unhealthy.

Get the Kids Involved

Tropical fish can be a great tool for educating your children about the environment and different varieties of fish and even procreation, but this isn't going to happen by chance.

Get the kids involved in the care of the fish and the tank. If the water gets a little green, talk to them about algae buildup and how that happens. Explain how we need to care for these things before they get worse and how important a healthy environment is for fish. If you can, let them pick out the fish they want to include in the tank. Observe how they interact with one another and point out the ones that are more shy and docile and the ones that are more aggressive.

Children typically care more for things that they are personally involved with, and this might include the fish and the tank. Just giving them the chore of cleaning the tank isn't going to make them appreciate the overall environment, but if they start to get personally involved with the fish they may care more about providing them with a healthy tank, and may not resent the chore so much. So get the kids involved and make your tank a true learning experience for everyone.

Give Your Fish an Occasional Treat

Never overfeed your fish; this cannot be emphasized enough. But an occasional treat here and there will relax them and make them feel more safe and secure.

So if you can afford it, get some live fish food or something frozen or freeze dried. Since you don't want to give it to them every day you can make it last for quite some time. But when you do give them a treat it can be a welcome change for them.

Be Prepared

Your fish are going to die eventually, so be prepared. Don't get panicked every time it happens and think you did something wrong. Some fish have very short life spans, so you may want to educate yourself on this when purchasing them so you know what to expect.

Have Fun!

This is probably the best advice we can give anyone when it comes to keeping tropical fish. This hobby is supposed to be fun and relaxing. Some claim that there are even physical benefits to watching fish, that it does actually relax and calm a person. Many who own fish will say this is true.

So in between the feeding, the cleaning, and the worrying if you're doing the right thing for them, try to schedule some time to just sit and enjoy them! Turn off the television and watch your aquarium for a little bit. Get to know your fish as individuals because that's what they are. Be determined to enjoy them just as much as you would any other pet, and really have some fun with your tropical fish!

Printed in Great Britain
by Amazon